T0413890

INSIDE MLS

VANCOUVER
WHITECAPS FC

BY CHRÖS MCDOUGALL

SportsZone

An Imprint of Abdo Publishing
abdobooks.com

abdobooks.com

Published by Abdo Publishing, a division of ABDO, PO Box 398166, Minneapolis, Minnesota 55439. Copyright © 2022 by Abdo Consulting Group, Inc. International copyrights reserved in all countries. No part of this book may be reproduced in any form without written permission from the publisher. SportsZone™ is a trademark and logo of Abdo Publishing.

Printed in the United States of America, North Mankato, Minnesota
052021
092021

THIS BOOK CONTAINS
RECYCLED MATERIALS

Cover Photo: Devin Manky/Icon Sportswire/AP Images
Interior Photos: Darryl Dyck/The Canadian Press/AP Images, 5, 6, 9, 10, 26, 29, 35, 39, 40, 43; Peter Robinson/EMPICS/PA Images/Getty Images, 13; Burnett/AP Images, 15; Eric Buermeyer/Shutterstock Images, 17; Sam Leung/The Canadian Press/AP Images, 18; Darryl Dyck/The Canadian Press/AP Images, 20; Joshua Weisberg/Icon SMI/Newscom, 22–23, 25; Jonathan Hayward/The Canadian Press/AP Images, 30; Alex Gallardo/AP Images, 32; Andy Clark/Reuters/Newscom, 36

Editor: Patrick Donnelly
Series Designer: Dan Peluso

Library of Congress Control Number: 2020948287

Publisher's Cataloging-in-Publication Data

Names: McDougall, Chrös, author.
Title: Vancouver Whitecaps FC / by Chrös McDougall
Description: Minneapolis, Minnesota : Abdo Publishing, 2022 | Series: Inside MLS | Includes online resources and index.
Identifiers: ISBN 9781532194832 (lib. bdg.) | ISBN 9781098214494 (ebook)
Subjects: LCSH: Vancouver Whitecaps FC (Soccer team)--Juvenile literature. | Soccer teams--Juvenile literature. | Professional sports franchises--Juvenile literature. | Sports Teams--Juvenile literature.
Classification: DDC 796.334--dc23

TABLE OF CONTENTS

CHAPTER 1

CHAMPIONS OF
CANADA

One by one, the fans made their way from the streets of downtown Vancouver into BC Place. Some brought giant flags. Many took their spots among likeminded supporters' groups. The Vancouver Whitecaps FC had been part of Major League Soccer (MLS) since 2011. But fans had been cheering on pro men's soccer in British Columbia's biggest city for decades. Now on August 26, 2015, a crowd of 19,616 eager fans showed up to cheer on the Whitecaps to their first Voyageurs Cup.

Awarded to Canada's national champion, the Voyageurs Cup was created in 2002. That was years before the country had any MLS teams. Since 2008, the trophy has gone to the winner of the annual Canadian Championship. And after

The Whitecaps' Russell Teibert, left, battles with the Impact's Johan Venegas during the second leg of the 2016 Canadian Championship final.

Getting around FC Edmonton in the Canadian Championship semifinals was no easy task for Nicolás Mezquida (9) and the Whitecaps.

five runner-up finishes, the 2015 Whitecaps were ready to make history.

TAKING ON CANADA'S BEST

Five teams took part in the 2015 Canadian Championship. Vancouver opened against FC Edmonton, a minor league team. It proved to be no minor task, though. After drawing at home,

BC PLACE

An older version of the Whitecaps was part of the North American Soccer League (NASL). They played their home games at BC Place when it opened in 1983. Nearly three decades later the team, now in MLS, moved back in. The stadium underwent major renovations after it was used for the 2010 Winter Olympics. The biggest change was replacing the air-supported dome with a retractable roof. After starting the 2011 season at Empire Field, the Whitecaps have called BC Place home since October of that year. The downtown stadium has also played host to major events, including the 2015 Women's World Cup final.

the Whitecaps needed a dramatic stoppage time goal on the road to secure a berth in the final.

That set up a home-and-home series against the Montreal Impact for the title. Like the Whitecaps, the Impact had once been a minor league team. They joined MLS in 2012, one year behind the Whitecaps. But going into the 2015 final, Montreal had won the Voyageurs Cup a record nine times, including in the previous two years.

On an August night in Montreal, the Whitecaps made their move. Darren Mattocks and Pedro Morales each scored to put Vancouver up 2–0. Then disaster struck. The Impact's Laurent Ciman cut the deficit to one in the 84th minute. One minute later, Anthony Jackson-Hamel tied it. Instead of a big

Fans play a major role at any MLS game, and Vancouver is no exception. The Whitecaps have four main supporters' groups. Their sections are often the loudest in the stadium. The groups also sometimes get together for away games or other activities outside of soccer. The Southsiders are the oldest and biggest of these groups. They have been around since 1999, when the team was still in a minor league.

road victory, the Whitecaps were coming home with the series deadlocked and momentum firmly on Montreal's side.

GAME TIME

Vancouver came out fast in the decisive second game. Kekuta Manneh had a chance from close range in the second minute. Montreal goalie Eric Kronberg stopped it. That was the first of many big saves for Kronberg.

In the 30th minute, the Whitecaps got their break. Montreal's Victor Cabrera tripped Octavio Rivero. That earned him a second yellow card, which meant he was ejected. The Impact were down to just 10 men for the rest of the game. And nine minutes after his takedown, Rivero got his revenge.

The Impact tried to play a ball back to Kronberg. Instead, Vancouver's Cristian Techera got to it first, taking possession right at the top of the box. Kronberg, scrambling to regain his positioning, was able to get a hand on Techera's shot, but he

Montreal defender Laurent Ciman (23) can only watch as Octavio Rivero
scores in the first half of their Voyageurs Cup showdown.

Vancouver's Gershon Koffie brings the 2015 Voyageurs Cup celebration to the fans at BC Place.

couldn't stop it. As the ball rolled across the goal line, Rivero blasted it into the netting. Vancouver was up 1–0.

Now Vancouver was in good position. Because the Whitecaps had scored twice on the road in the first game,

Montreal would need to either win this game or score at least three goals in a draw in order to claim the championship. Both paths suddenly looked a whole lot steeper.

Just after halftime, the Whitecaps all but turned that pathway into a cliff when Tim Parker headed in a goal off a corner kick to put his team up 2–0. That's how things ended. The Whitecaps had won 4–2 on aggregate to claim the tournament title. Midfielder Russell Teibert, an Ontario native, was named most valuable player. His efforts helped keep Montreal from landing a single shot on goal.

"It's our time now and we showed that tonight," Teibert said. "There was never any question that we were going to win this game."

CHAPTER 2

A LONG
HISTORY

A hard rain fell in western Canada as the San Jose Earthquakes and the Vancouver Whitecaps made their way onto the field at Empire Stadium. Soccer had been played in Canada as far back as the 1870s. Now, a century later, professional men's soccer was sweeping across North America. And so on May 5, 1974, the Whitecaps debuted in the NASL.

It wasn't an ideal start. San Jose took the lead just three minutes into the game. However, Whitecaps defender Neil Ellett tied it up before halftime—his goal being the first in team history. Ultimately the game had to be settled by a shootout, and after a marathon 19 rounds, the Earthquakes prevailed. Nonetheless, the Whitecaps era had begun.

Vancouver's Alan Ball (23) and Buzz Parsons (7) took on the Tampa Bay Rowdies in Soccer Bowl '79.

BEFORE THE WHITECAPS

The NASL's Whitecaps weren't Vancouver's first pro soccer team. In fact they weren't even Vancouver's first NASL team. A team called the Vancouver Royals played one season in the NASL, finishing last in 1968. Ferenc Puskás, a former superstar for Hungary, served as manager. The first-ever pro soccer game to take place in Vancouver was between teams called the Rovers and Callies in March 1910.

As the NASL took hold, some of the most famous players from around the world came to North America to be a part of it. This only helped the league grow further. While the biggest names went to other teams, most notably the New York Cosmos, Vancouver quietly put together a strong team.

Built around a strong defense and several Canadian players, the Whitecaps reached the playoffs in 1976, 1977, and 1978. In 1979 everything came together. The team had talented players, such as English goalie Phil Parkes and midfielder Alan Ball. The latter had even played in two World Cups for England, winning one. But no one player dominated.

"This is a team, not a collection of stars," Ball said. "A team."

Fans embraced that squad as it upset the Cosmos in the playoffs to qualify for the league championship game, which was called the Soccer Bowl. Around 50,000 fans showed up to

Vancouver's Kevin Hector, *left*, battles with Vladislav Bogicevic of the New York Cosmos during a 1979 NASL playoff game.

watch the Whitecaps face the Tampa Bay Rowdies at Giants Stadium near New York City. Parkes was on top of his game, stopping two all-but-certain Rowdies goals. Meanwhile, Trevor Whymark scored twice and Vancouver won 2–1.

The Soccer Bowl victory made the Whitecaps the first professional team from Vancouver to win a major sports title. More than 100,000 fans lined Granville Street for the team's victory parade. The sun beat down on the players as they showed off their shiny new trophy.

The future looked bright for soccer across North America and especially in Vancouver. The Whitecaps continued to draw big crowds. As many as 30,000 came out to each home game in 1983. However, both the league and the team were struggling to make money. Following the 1984 season, the NASL folded.

PLAY ON

The end of the NASL didn't spell the end of soccer in Canada or in Vancouver. In 1986 a new league formed called the Canadian Soccer League. The Vancouver 86ers were charter members as the league began play the next year. The team was named in honor of the city's founding year (1886), the club's founding year (1986), and the Canada men's national team reaching the 1986 World Cup. Today's Whitecaps trace back to this team.

Over the next quarter century, the team underwent various changes. It jumped from one league to another multiple times. In 2000 the 86ers changed identities, bringing back the Whitecaps name. The name is a tribute to the natural beauty of the area. In 1973 Danny Veitch, one of the NASL team's original owners, came up with it while driving across the Lions Gate Bridge. On one side of the bridge were big waves, called

According to legend, a drive across Vancouver's Lions Gate Bridge inspired the Whitecaps nickname.

English superstar David Beckham of the LA Galaxy evades the Whitecaps' Tony Donatelli during their 2007 friendly at BC Place.

whitecaps, on the ocean. On the other side, he saw a different kind of whitecaps—snow atop the nearby mountains.

The team experienced periods of success during this minor league era. It even won a few championships. Four came during the early CSL years. The new Whitecaps added two more titles in 2006 and 2008. By then, however, soccer was once again growing in popularity across North America. The Whitecaps were preparing to take the next step.

BACK TO THE BIG LEAGUE

On January 11, 2007, the Los Angeles Galaxy shocked sports fans. David Beckham, the English midfielder and one of the most popular athletes in the world, was coming to MLS. Interest in MLS spiked. In November of that year, the Whitecaps invited Beckham and the Galaxy to Vancouver for a friendly. A crowd of 48,172 showed up to watch at BC Place.

At the same time, MLS was expanding. Toronto FC became the league's first Canadian team in 2007. The next year, a new San Jose Earthquakes returned to MLS, and in 2009 the Seattle Sounders followed. Toronto and Vancouver were natural rivals in other sports. Meanwhile, Vancouver soccer teams had been facing opponents from San Jose and Seattle in other leagues for years.

Vancouver's Pedro Morales hoists the Cascadia Cup after the Whitecaps won it in October 2016.

CASCADIA CUP

Some of MLS' most intense games take place between its three teams from the Cascadia region in the Pacific Northwest. Although the Whitecaps and Portland Timbers joined MLS in 2011, two years after the Seattle Sounders did, pro soccer in this region goes back even before MLS began in 1996. Teams from the three cities—using the same names—first met in the 1970s during the NASL era. In 2004, when the teams were part of the same minor league, fans created the Cascadia Cup. It's still awarded each season to the team with the best results against the other two.

Everything appeared in place for Vancouver to take the step to follow its peers to MLS. On March 18, 2009, it became official. The Whitecaps would join the league in 2011. And soon they learned they would do so alongside another longtime rival, the Portland Timbers.

CHAPTER 3

TIP OF THE
WHITECAPS

Jay DeMerit arrived in Vancouver in 2011 with a well-earned reputation. A native of Wisconsin, he had found after leaving college in 2003 that no MLS teams were interested in him. So he packed up and caught a flight to England. He was determined to make it as a professional soccer player. Over seven seasons there, he did that and then some.

A central defender, DeMerit started near the bottom. His first opportunity came in England's ninth tier, a long way from the famous Premier League. DeMerit earned just $70 a week and slept in a friend's attic. But the more he worked, the more he got noticed. Within a year, he earned a trial with Watford in the second division. That led to a contract, and in his second season with Watford, DeMerit headed in the goal

Defender Jay DeMerit brought veteran savvy and toughness to the Whitecaps.

VANCOUVER STALWARTS

Jordan Harvey joined the Whitecaps before their first MLS season in 2011. Over the next seven seasons, the left back proved to be one of the team's most consistent players. When he left to join his hometown Los Angeles FC in 2018, he held the club records for all-time MLS starts, appearances, and minutes played. Not far behind him in each category, however, was midfielder Russell Teibert. The Ontario native also was part of the inaugural 2011 team, and he was still with the Whitecaps in 2021.

that secured the team's promotion into the Premier League.

DeMerit ended up playing six seasons for Watford, including that memorable 2006–07 campaign in the Premier League. Along the way, he earned a spot on the US men's national team. In 2010 he started all four games for the US team at the World Cup in South Africa.

Not long after, however, he decided he wanted to come home to North America. In the Whitecaps, he found the perfect fit. The team was getting ready to join MLS, and it was looking for gritty, hard-working players like DeMerit to lead the way. So the Whitecaps not only made him their first MLS signing, they also named him team captain.

"It's a great challenge to lead the club from the start," DeMerit said. "That's what I was brought to Vancouver to do, and that's what I plan to do."

Jay DeMerit, *right*, and Jordan Harvey keep the Seattle Sounders away from their goal during a 2013 game.

On March 19, 2011—eight years after every MLS team passed on him —DeMerit made his MLS debut. At 31 years old, he was a veteran player. He provided steady leadership to the growing team during its early years. In 2012 he became the first Whitecaps player to earn a spot in the MLS All-Star Game. However, injuries wiped out most of his 2013 season, and

Alphonso Davies, *right*, dribbles away from an Orlando City defender during his MLS debut in July 2016.

2014 was looking like more of the same. That, he decided, was reason to officially end one of the most remarkable careers in North American soccer.

"I've never taken the field just because I can," he wrote in a letter to fans. "I'm either all in or all out."

TEENAGE SENSATION

Alphonso Davies was just 13 years old when Whitecaps scouts first spotted him. The son of Liberian parents, Davies was born in a refugee camp in Ghana and moved to Canada with his family at age five. They eventually settled in Edmonton, where he went from participating in a free after-school soccer program to becoming a star on his youth teams. That's when the Whitecaps invited him to move farther west. In August 2015, Davies joined the Whitecaps' youth residency program in Vancouver.

The teenager spent just over three years with the organization, but what a memorable three years they were. Blazing fast and technically gifted, the winger played his first MLS game in July 2016. At 15 years old, he was the second-youngest MLS player ever.

By 2017 Davies was making regular appearances for the Whitecaps. The next year, at just 17, he was a regular starter. Despite his age, he used his speed and strength to hold his own against much older players. He could play both an attacking role and a wingback role that required more defensive responsibilities. All of this caught the attention of

Germany's biggest team, Bayern Munich. It paid an MLS-record transfer fee of $13.5 million to get him.

Davies stayed in Vancouver until the end of the season, and he made it count. The teenager played in his first All-Star Game that summer. Then, just before Halloween, more than 25,000 fans showed up at BC Place to send him off. Davies left them with some memories. In the 28th minute, he collected the ball around midfield, dribbled to the top of the penalty area, and then blasted a shot past Portland's goalkeeper. Just three minutes later, he stole the ball near Portland's goal and chipped it in. They were his seventh and eighth goals of the season, to go with 11 assists. They also helped the Whitecaps end the season with a 2–1 win.

"Coming in this game, knowing it's my last game for Vancouver," Davies said, "I just wanted to leave with a positive feeling."

STRIKE FORCE

Every team needs a go-to scorer, and the Whitecaps have had many. Camilo Sanvezzo set the standard. The Brazilian striker, known just as Camilo, made his first Whitecaps start in April 2011. He ended the game with two goals and an assist in a 3–3 home draw against Sporting Kansas City.

Alphonso Davies and his family pose for photos ahead of his final game with the Whitecaps in October 2018.

Whitecaps fans got used to seeing forward Camilo celebrate goals during the 2013 season.

Camilo stayed in British Columbia for just three seasons, but he left with no shortage of accolades. He led all Whitecaps players with 12 goals in 2011, then added five more in 2012. However, it was in 2013 when he really left his mark. The skilled striker came into the league's final game with 19 goals. He ended the season with an MLS-best 22 after scoring a hat trick in a 3–0 win, sending beloved teammate Young-Pyo Lee into retirement on a high note.

"Throughout a long season it takes a consistent goal scorer to win the Golden Boot," DeMerit said. "These things are not by fluke."

THE GREATEST GOALIE

One goalkeeper in Whitecaps history stands above the rest. David Ousted joined the team in 2013 and was the primary starter until late in the 2017 season. During that time, the native of Denmark established just about every MLS-era goalkeeping record for the Whitecaps, including total wins, saves, and shutouts. His play was key for the Whitecaps during the 2015 season in which they reached the playoffs and won the Canadian Championship.

Unfortunately, the Camilo era ended after that when the player and club couldn't agree on a new contract. However, several other productive goal-scorers followed. Before the next season, the team signed Chilean forward Pedro Morales. He too stayed just three seasons, but during that time he followed

The Whitecaps brought in Lucas Cavallini (9) to be their next great striker in 2020.

DeMerit as the second captain in team history. Morales also made his mark on the scoresheet, especially in 2014. Going into 2020, only Camilo had scored more than Morales's 25 goals for the Whitecaps, but no Vancouver player had racked up more assists than the Chilean's 22.

However, Fredy Montero surpassed Morales to become the Whitecaps' second leading scorer in 2020. The Colombian forward, who had formerly starred for the Seattle Sounders, joined the Whitecaps on loan for the 2017 season. He promptly scored a team-high 13 regular-season goals in leading the Whitecaps back to the playoffs. So two years later, the team signed the 5-foot-9 striker outright. After Montero again led the team with eight goals in 2019, the team paired him with newcomer Lucas Cavallini to form a dangerous attack in 2020. The duo lived up to the hype. Canada native Cavallini led all Whitecaps players with six goals, while Montero was just behind him with five goals plus a team-leading five assists.

CHAPTER 4

MAKING WAVES

Brisk spring air and soft blue skies greeted captain Jay DeMerit as he led the Whitecaps, dressed in their classic white uniforms, onto the field on March 19, 2011. Basketball star Steve Nash, a co-owner of the team, banged a drum. An overflow crowd of more than 22,000 fans cheered with him as they awaited the city's first top-division soccer game since the 1980s.

"I just feel like a superfan," said Nash, a native of nearby Victoria. "I have been a Whitecaps fan since I was a little boy. To see us back in the top flight in North America is exciting. The atmosphere is great. It makes a really great day."

The Whitecaps soon made it even better. Facing off against Toronto FC, they came out fast. Just 15 minutes in,

Vancouver native Terry Dunfield celebrates with the home crowd after scoring in the Whitecaps' MLS debut.

Captain Jay DeMerit leads the Whitecaps onto Empire Field for the team's first MLS game in 2011.

Eric Hassli scored the first goal in the team's MLS history when he knocked the ball off the far post and into the net.

Toronto quickly answered, only to see Terry Dunfield put the home team up once again in the 26th minute. The Vancouver native was so thrilled he jumped into the stands, a celebration that earned him a yellow card. From there it was all Vancouver. Atiba Harris added another goal in the 63rd minute, and nine minutes later Hassli scored again to put it out of reach. Although Toronto added a late goal, Vancouver held on to win its first MLS match 4–2.

The memorable day at Empire Field offered a sign of what could be in Vancouver. It also started a tradition. The Whitecaps have opened every MLS season at home. And they won their first four season openers.

A TWO-YEAR RUN

Across four seasons in MLS, the Whitecaps had shown improvement. They went from last place in 2011 to making the playoffs twice in the next three years. In 2015 they were ready to take the next step. The team brought in talented Uruguayans Octavio Rivero, a forward, and center back Diego Rodriguez. They joined veterans such as midfielder Pedro Morales, defender Kendall Waston, and

PLAYOFF BOUND

As summer turned to fall in 2012, the Whitecaps found themselves in the mix for the last Western Conference playoff spot. However, the second-year team was in free fall. It ended the season with just one win in its last 10 games. That win was a big one, though, with Vancouver beating Chivas USA 4–0. In the end it proved enough to get the Whitecaps the last playoff berth. That made them the first Canadian team to reach the MLS playoffs.

goalkeeper Davis Ousted. The pieces were in place for the Whitecaps' best season yet.

"Everyone's fit, everyone's hungry," defender Steven Beitashour said. "We're just counting down the days until [opening day], so we're excited and ready to go."

Although the Whitecaps lost their opener—their first time doing that—they came back to win four straight matches. That set the tone for a 16–13–5 season, marking the third-best record in the entire league. The MLS season ended in disappointment when the Portland Timbers held the Whitecaps scoreless over two games in the Western Conference semifinals. However, a development earlier in the season set the stage for more success to come.

That August, the Whitecaps had beaten the Montreal Impact to win their first Canadian Championship. That in turn secured Vancouver a spot in the 2016–17 Concacaf Champions League, a tournament featuring the best teams from the region. And competing in the Champions League for the second year in a row, the Whitecaps got hot.

In the group stage, they swept all four games against Sporting Kansas City and Central FC, a team from Trinidad & Tobago. That sent Vancouver into the quarterfinals against

Whitecaps fans were ready for their club to make a run in the 2016–17 Concacaf Champions League.

the top seed. Up next was a showdown with the New York Red Bulls.

The Whitecaps struck first. Kekuta Manneh scored on a header off a corner kick to open the scoring in the February 2017 meeting at Red Bull Arena. Ousted stopped a penalty kick a few minutes later. Although New York's Bradley Wright-Phillips scored to secure a 1–1 tie, the Whitecaps left in

The Whitecaps' Alphonso Davies lines up to shoot against Tigres in the 2017 Champions League semifinals.

a strong position. Because away goals are used as a tiebreaker, they could advance with a win or 0–0 tie at home in the second leg.

No tiebreakers were needed. Alphonso Davies, the Whitecaps' teenage star, faked out a defender before calmly placing the ball into the open net in the fifth minute. A few big saves from Ousted kept New York off the scoresheet. Then, in the 76th minute, Fredy Montero sealed it. In his first game for the club, Montero came off the bench and blasted a bouncing ball off his laces from just beyond the penalty spot. The keeper got a hand on it, but there was little he could do to stop the ball from going into the back of the net.

The 3–1 aggregate win made Vancouver just the seventh MLS team to reach the Champions League semifinals. There, however, they went up against Tigres, a powerful team from Mexico. After falling 2–0 in the first leg in Monterrey, Mexico, the Whitecaps had a tough hill to climb. Midfielder Brek Shea got that started with a goal just three minutes into the return match in Vancouver. However, Shea was then injured two minutes later. Two second-half goals from Tigres ended the Whitecaps' run.

"There's nothing to be ashamed of in that locker room there," coach Carl Robinson said after the game. "We've gone toe-to-toe, and we've just come up a little bit short."

SHAKING THE QUAKES

The Whitecaps were back in the hunt for another trophy when the 2017 MLS playoffs began in October. Their first-round match against San Jose went scoreless for the first half hour. Then, in the 33rd minute, a corner kick found Kendall Waston right in front of the Earthquakes' goal. He headed the ball toward the far post to Montero, who headed it into the goal. Just like that, the rout was on.

Cristian Techera was next. The skillful winger curled a hard, 30-yard free kick into the top corner in the 57th minute. Waston banged in a rebound seven minutes later to make it 3–0. Then it was Nicolás Mezquida's turn. The substitute knocked in a pair of goals in the 78th and 80th minutes. The 21,083 rowdy fans at BC Place roared with each one. And they had good reason.

Since joining MLS, the Whitecaps had never scored five goals in one game in any competition. Only one game in MLS Cup playoffs history had been decided by more than five goals. And, most importantly, the knockout round win meant Vancouver was advancing in the MLS Cup playoffs for the first time. Though they lost to Seattle in the next round, the victory over San Jose gave fans reason to celebrate and hope for more big moments to come.

"You saw what it meant to the players and the club," Robinson said of their playoff success. "We were so determined to get that first playoff win, and we did. Did we do it in style? Yeah, we probably did."

Kendall Waston (4) celebrates with Fredy Montero after scoring in the Whitecaps' record 2017 playoff win over San Jose.

TIMELINE

1974	1987	2010	2011	2012
The original Vancouver Whitecaps debut in the NASL. The Whitecaps win the league's 1979 championship, but the NASL folds following the 1984 season.	A new Vancouver soccer team plays its first game. Originally called the Vancouver 86ers, this team would play in various minor leagues over the coming years before joining MLS in 2011.	Jay DeMerit signs as the first Whitecaps player of the MLS era, and he goes on to become the first team captain as well.	The Whitecaps begin their MLS era with a 4–2 win over rivals Toronto FC at Empire Field in Vancouver.	Vancouver goes 11–13–10, but most importantly the Whitecaps become the first Canadian team to reach the MLS playoffs.

2013	2015	2016	2017	2018
Brazilian forward Camilo scores a hat trick in the season finale to boost his total to 22 goals and win the league's Golden Boot.	Vancouver defeats the Montreal Impact to win its first Canadian Championship.	The Whitecaps sweep through the group stage of the Concacaf Champions League and then defeat the New York Red Bulls to advance to the semifinals.	The Whitecaps win their first playoff game in record-setting fashion, defeating the San Jose Earthquakes 5–0 in the knockout round.	Teenager Alphonso Davies wraps up his short career in Vancouver with two goals in his final game before joining German team Bayern Munich on an MLS-record

TEAM FACTS

FIRST SEASON

2011

STADIUM

Empire Field (2011)
BC Place (2011–)

CANADIAN CHAMPIONSHIP TITLES

2015

KEY PLAYERS

Camilo (2011–13)
Lucas Cavallini (2020–)
Maxime Crépeau (2019–)
Alphonso Davies (2016–18)
Jay DeMerit (2011–14)
Jordan Harvey (2011–17)
Young-Pyo Lee (2012–13)
Fredy Montero (2017, 2019–)
Pedro Morales (2014–16)
David Ousted (2013–17)
Russell Teibert (2011–)
Kendall Waston (2014–18)

KEY COACHES

Carl Robinson (2014–18)
Marc Dos Santos (2019–)

MLS GOLDEN BOOT

Camilo (2013)

MLS GOAL OF THE YEAR

Camilo (2013)

MLS NEWCOMER OF THE YEAR

Pedro Morales (2014)

GLOSSARY

aggregate
The combined score of both games in a two-game series.

contract
An agreement between a player and team that determines how much the player will be paid and for how long.

friendly
A game that is not part of an official competition.

leg
One game that is part of a series of games.

promotion
To move up to a higher division. In some countries, the teams that finish atop the standings move up to the next division for the following season.

refugee camp
A temporary settlement for people who have been forced to leave their country, often due to war or harmful treatment from the government.

transfer fee
A set amount of money that one teams pays another in order to obtain rights to a player.

scouts
People who study other players, teams, or both on behalf of a given team.

stoppage time
Time the referee adds to the end of each half to account for stoppages in play, such as for injuries.

supporters' groups
Fan groups that stand and support their team throughout the game by singing, chanting, drumming, waving flags, and more.

veteran
A player with a lot of experience.

MORE INFORMATION

BOOKS

Kortemeier, Todd. *Total Soccer*. Minneapolis, MN: Abdo Publishing, 2017.

Marthaler, Jon. *Ultimate Soccer Road Trip*. Minneapolis, MN: Abdo Publishing, 2019.

McDougall, Chrös. *Toronto FC*. Minneapolis, MN: Abdo Publishing, 2022.

ONLINE RESOURCES

To learn more about the Vancouver Whitecaps FC, please visit **abdobooklinks.com** or scan this QR code. These links are routinely monitored and updated to provide the most current information available.

INDEX

ABOUT THE AUTHOR

Chrös McDougall is a sportswriter and children's book author. A lifelong soccer fan, he covered the opening of England's Wembley Stadium for the Associated Press and has been following Major League Soccer since the mid-2000s. McDougall lives in Minneapolis with his wife, two kids, and boxer, Eira.